Selected Poems

Irene Mitchell

FUTURECYCLE PRESS

www.futurecycle.org

Library of Congress Control Number: 2021930898

Published by FutureCycle Press
Athens, GA

ISBN 978-1-952593-16-1

Contents

Foreword

from
CLERESTORY

from
FEVER

from
EQUAL PARTS SUN AND SHADE:
AN ALMANAC OF PRECARIOUS DAYS

from
MINDING THE SPECTRUM'S BUSINESS

from
A STUDY OF EXTREMES IN SIX SUITES

from
SEA WIND ON THE WHITE PILLOW

Foreword

Lyric poetry is an expression of literary art that is at once personal and universal, elevating a viewpoint through image and language. It is a kind of song, originating in *lyre*, the Greek word for a melodious stringed instrument; how apt for a poet who collaborates with artists and composers to choose this form to speak to her readers.

Irene Mitchell and I met some years ago when I was teaching publishing classes at The New School and advising the participants on where to send their poems for publication. When I read hers, I spotted a lyric voice I thought would fit in a particular university journal publishing out of Boston. We conversed about the power and flexibility of the lyric, and I am pleased to see that she has been composing her sublime existential songs through several collections.

We are living in an America, twenty years into the new millennium, where veracity has been challenged, and insult and lies posted on social platforms are refreshed by the second, even if our energy is not. Where can we turn to find ourselves renewed and addressed? The lyric is the balm, and with Mitchell's curiosity and literacy, a wresting of power from destruction.

> If one could siphon energy
> from catastrophe,
> harmony from ruin,
> there would be left a rich little world
> of dignity and sharp ideas.
> —from *Swizzle Stick*

Mitchell is a poet who desires irregularity over repetition, "pulverizing/ phrases until the pith is refined/and resonates." She has drawn poems from six collections and pulls out a pocketful of new lyrics to entice you into a selection that, much like her literary hero, Emily Dickinson, has her surveying whatever abounds. In her cosmic leaps, wit and wonder share the stage with conflict. She has described her poetic formula as "scrutiniz(ing) the discordant, as well as the harmonious notes, to see what fits." Mitchell will lift you out of the clamor of our current discordance, and make you feel refreshed. I am certain you will find clarity and complexity in this abundant and uplifting selection.

—Amy Holman

Amy Holman is a Pushcart Prize-nominated poet and prose writer, a literary consultant, and artist. She is the author of the collection *Wrens Fly Through the Open Window* (Somondoco Press, 2010) and four chapbooks, including the prize-winning *Wait for Me, I'm Gone* (Dream Horse Press, 2005). She teaches frequently at the Hudson Valley Writers Center and lives in Brooklyn, New York.

for
Helen and Carolyn

I lie abstracted and hear beautiful tales of things and the reasons of things,
They are so beautiful I nudge myself to listen....
And that I can think such thoughts as these is just as wonderful,
And that I can remind you, and you think them and know them to be
*   true, is just as wonderful.*

—Walt Whitman, "Who Learns My Lesson Complete?"

from
CLERESTORY

(Dos Madres Press, 2020)

The Intervals

How are the intervals filled
without a story to tell?
They are filled with deeds.
You have your practice and I have mine.

I had a whole, hard world
of time in which to deliver,
receiving fringe benefits
and company perks
such as a jacket with an inside pocket.

There was also the tasty aftermath
of earnings,
green peppercorns ground
to satisfaction for a dish.

I found others nearby
also busy at their work.
I greet the divine in them
for they labored long
and fruitfully without capitalizing
on conflict in their story.

You may not wish to hear my story,
for as soon as I'd begin to reveal
a detail, you might look away
to see who else
has entered the room.

Nevertheless, since fortune has given me
access to fresh air and ambient light,
I will circulate some particulars
about my days and deeds,
for that is what it is to be alive.

Who Reads Dante?

Who, standing here, is not ready
to take on the next moment,
for being alive
means searching
for such satisfactions as there may be,
exclusive of conflict or complaint.

My complaint
is that the cataract of time,
being heedless, explains little
about how to separate the photograph
from the actual
or the stars from their mooring.
Who, standing here, cares anything
about my particular set of quandaries,
anyway,
how I blush to admit
or thwart
infiltrating disturbances on any given day.

In the long run, I am happy
if I hit a chord among the crowd
or with even one person who beckons
to come along, a companion,
as together we advance through the next
precious moment, wending our way
through the spiral, toward the pinnacle.

Visit from a Raptor of Interest

Let me not waste myself on impossible flights....
—William Everson

A hawk presents nearby,
the elm's limb so close
to the window I think
it has come to visit me in camaraderie.

I left the city for the night air here,
the hawks and hilarious jumping rabbits,
the cricket concerts,
the black of the berry.
Here, there isn't much to be distressed about.
One day there is algae in the pond,
gone the next day and the water lively again.

I have named the hawk Ted
for its poetic input, the language
of its muscles, the holding at the back
of a few grey feathers,
the wingspan huge
even, I suppose, in the rain.
Goodbye, Ted.

Heeding cautions and riptides,
where this bird goes, there go I
into the wind
and overwhelming sky.

Milk in a Dish

Now to go from A to B
joyously. Unless A is jealous
of B.
Try to avoid that situation
and proceed softly
as a willow engaged in its breeze.

Of all the compensations
to choose from, lightness is choice—
unless brooding brings the depth
you are searching for.

Also in high regard among qualities
is curiosity.
Long may it live as a lifeline.
Be prepared to delay dying
because there are many curiosities, cat,
still to satisfy.

Alouette

I say, *Most injurious to the mind is repetition,*
the constant tapping of the hammer upon the copper rail.

You say, *Let's go rowing,*
and that, at first, seems sporting and unusual.
We do it every summer day
and there are over sixty of those,
until the sight of the boat, the feel of the oar
becomes as dull as the vision of the same rowers
skirting the same edge in the same pond.
If only one would topple and create a different eddy.

Where is Home?

Hours empty into the ether.
The pond, which carries my hat downstream,
is still.
This is my metaphor for
the looming end.

Until then, may the pond flow gently
for morning is here.
Birds pass by and often linger.
For the work to be done today
vigor is needed.
To surpass the previous day's
assignment, muscle is key.
Alleluia for any extra effort!

A pink cloud scuds over the birch
I planted when I moved here.
I witnessed that another birch
appeared next to it, until a whole forest
came of it.

I often walk through stands
of trim birch shining and thriving
amidst the divine.
There I find evidence
where the birch is thickest
of constant talk among them.
I am invited to join in any time.

But I venture home
to put up the tea
and save my breath to cool my porridge.

Useless Worries

Fortune favors the brave.
—Pliny the Elder, AD 79

These worries send a chill
which will crest until I change my mind
about what is dreary here.

I compare my worries
to those the sky is tasked with:
when to dispense rain,
when to order wind to kick up,
when to get the fire crackling,
when to shine the moon.

*What did you hear
and to what purpose?*

I heard night noises
(which I suspect are weeds
destroying the garden).
I heard the toneless echoes
of woodpeckers tapping on old bark.
I waited for the phone to ring
(as is its function)
but it was silent
so I waited for the vexing dough to rise.

I heard through Pliny the Younger
that Pliny the Elder
suffocated in fallen ash and pumice
from Vesuvius' eruption
while trying to rescue friends
and reassure them
there was nothing to worry about.
We know how that turned out.

Dream Gazette II

There was plenty of plotting
against the cold,
and little celebration for its cohort,
ice under cover of snow.
So let us drink now to the last of winter
depending upon which spot in the universe
you are reviewing.

From my spot right here, the days
and nights spring sweet and generous
as a goblet filled with port.

I celebrate with a practiced plunge
into Caribbean waters, and witness squid
navigating toward moonlight.
Everything is upward
and extending.

I swim to the shoreline
where trees are full of fruit,
each seed a ripening grape.

Presto,
an archer aimed his bow.
I checked my vulnerable limbs and hide
for the accuracy of his mark
and found that I was wounded.
He had pierced my Eden
and pitched it into the void.

Trinity

All the jonquils were in a row.
She looked up from her planting
to find the woman next to her
still digging. That woman
looked up from her digging
at the woman to her left
who had hours ago finished
her rows and was now contemplating
how comfortable the jonquils looked
in the garden as a whole.

This trinity of planters
is in reality a painted image.
It depicts the last woman
in a vanishing aura, a breeze perhaps,
meant to keep her in the garden
a bit longer.

I could name the three women
if I thought it would have meaning
for anyone but the three of us.

The Kick

At the sight of the gorge
the pulse quickens
because there the rapids begin.
The river's history has long
been plotted and recorded
so its continuum is not a care
except for what can be gleaned
from the cascade's roar.

I am looking here for a theme
that hasn't yet been tampered with:
not grief, loss, or sorrow;
not satisfaction, completion, renewal.
I do not want to dwell on marvels
or reminiscences about the last of a tribe.
I have used these themes before,
giving up all my secrets
to the posse.

I'll lose a gunfight
for a theme that has ramifications
though they may hurt.
If the interest lies in negatives
while positives go begging,
there's a theme right there
and it's a peach:
Who is wearing my wool?
ponders the sheep,
scuffing its germinal territory.

Clerestory

The light burns early—
a standard rescue when rescue
is needed from November's slow
marauding across the browning hills.
Here and there bush and bittersweet
intrude if only to flatter solitude.

There is no trend to this winding down
but what I give it, no string
to draw or loosen
before my next anticipated entry
into one more night among thousands
of a fair existence spent
minding the firmament's business.
No buildings or lectures to endure,
only the bare sky of an invisible city.

Exquisite

I was far away
and now am close.
Hopes are rounding
to a moon's fullness
and its light, as well.
All hellish quandaries
descend to their fiery origins
and vaporize, not to be called back.

This is a happy turn
as my travels will bear out
for I am greeted heartily
everywhere, whether the place
is spare or sparse, whether or not
the sky is wholly exquisite.

I have always known
how to study rarities,
never tiring of searching for them.
So have you done the same
during your stay.

Morning Prayers Beginning with I

Early morning
knows how to land a blow
and I know how to take it.
I spring up, noticing
a sudden pain in the ear.

I question whether everyone else
carrying gear
is moody and so affected
by morning's unclassified disorder.

I tune in, abiding by the order
to take what fits
and not be blamed.
Confidentially, this is a tense business,
the avoidance of conflict.

As I tire of minor afflictions
so do they tire of me.
I say morning prayers solemnly,
not in a creak of a voice
but with fervor and inclusion.

I have plenty of references
in my aspirations arsenal
which I can elevate above the heart
on this forgiving morning
when there is birdsong in the distance
to conduct the hours smoothly
and the unregulated chimes
of far-off spires
to bring the world I desire
closer than imagined.

The Less Lonely Perimeter

The colder the night, the faster
I run past lamplight's curtain,
pace the only constant, the only race
my own against day's dawning.

The quiet is deeper at daybreak,
more cavernous.
Sky an abrupt, early white.

In the awaking dawn, a missionary
appears who I am pleased to meet
for our discussion is overdue.

We do not get dreamy or digress
as we exchange discoveries.
Our speech is without twists or tangles,
our bodies light
as a hammock slung beneath two poplars.

By and by our conversation reveals
that the cavern has a trap door
and lingo can go
only so far.

I have heard that contemplation
of the elsewhere
may fend off the darks and damps
of lingering loneliness, unveiling all the beauty
poured out for us each day.

Deconstruction

Why preserve a rose in a book
or even cut its stem!
You needn't summon memory
to know
that each rose lives
to find the night and heed the day.
Its thorns should never
have let you touch it.

A Cricket Calls

When a cricket calls I go
to the field of asters and drooping goldenrod
where wily bees hide, making hay
of the day.
Shall I chase this bee
before it comes to me
striped and silly, in a mood?

I am my own advocate in this regard
so I leave the bees to their cares.

They are unaware that I sense
their hidden pleasures,
that I have discovered their flowery homes
which they have invaded
with no notion of consequence or prison
or a room without a window,
or of being accused of something
sometime,
apart from menacing a bare bum.

How the Lines Fit Together

A closer look at the fabric
reveals that the spider
is a worthy architect.
That fact does not require
further investigation
unless one wants to copy
how lines lead out from the center
in a pattern that cannot be duplicated.
In the end, one may write an abstract
about the neat perimeter
and what the spider may have had in mind.

To dwell on one's own lines
as the architect of one's own days
is another worthy theme,
presupposing that plenty of time is on tap
to manage how the lines
should circumnavigate the whole
before dissolving.

The Art of Revision

The consuming nature of this art
is one in which confidence plays a part.
To those who say the work's
too dense, or metaphysical,
too chic or academic,
I respond with sweet composure

that fruits selected for the bowl
will in their sweet insolence
show that they can plump by dinner's end,
spiffy in their marinade, and with confidence
be laid as art
upon the poet's inner table.

Identity

My double said to me,
I am offering you adventure
beyond your wildest dream of idleness.

Then I, who love idleness,
retreated to consider this proposal.

Having considered, I received another
offering from my double,
this time for compensation
beyond my fondest dream of avarice.

It came in the form of confirmation
from the universe
that all my nouns and verbs
would be forever soluble
in the pervading mixture
of light and air.

I like the woods to be full
of squirrels and rabbits.
They don't like idleness,
ceaselessly on the run
within their realm.
Nor do they care for avarice,
taking only their allotted
portion of grasses, nuts, and seeds.

Scenery

The snow has seemingly settled
to a state of lifelong lingering.
I would travel away even by scurvy boat
to the rainforest
so humid that drops fall all day
down broad leaves,
tremulous and shining.

That would be my repair
unless there I should meet a jaguar.
It is fair to suppose I might.

However, I am here and have options,
preferring light entertainment
such as organizing the rubble
of my room.
Finding promises lying within,
I feel mighty.
I am going to scour the floor
and part the curtains.

Thoughts, Not Stories

Thoughts, not stories
will get me into Heaven.

I think, therefore I don't know
where thoughts will lead
except to more,
but they will be originals.

I don't mean to imply
all my thoughts are unique,
but they seem satisfying
in a comforting, personal way,
full of angles and breadth.
As for width,
there are many inherent angles
making the right moves tricky.

For example, how can I hurry
a poem along, knowing
there is an anthem in a word;
why would I paint a wall
without primer
knowing that a crack may appear
in an adjacent wall.

The instructions advise:
allow one shade
to build upon another
until oils are overrun
with flamboyant possibility.
In the current glare
some of that paint
will naturally permeate.

The Far View

Then comes night, under cover
of constellations, the nearer each star
the more blistering.

Then springs morning, borne of night's
strict reliance on forgiveness
for the demands and mistakes
wrought by day.

To make real what has been imagined
is to finish the plot,
whether looking years back, or to now,
making sure that the ground and the mind
are linked.

I have learned this
sitting and watching from the clerestory
where perception is edgy, vain, ancestral.

The Last Station

The topic concerned the stations
of a life and how one could choose
to revisit any
and mark them significant.

It was decided that the stations
worth discussing
were those that informed one's life,
generating pivotal beams
which charted a course.

Many stations at first came to mind
from the mainstream,
the strongest pulled to safety on the shore
as survivors,
and there they sunned upon the sand.

The stations were revealed
as actual places and actual people:
the house, the school, the voyages, the loves—
never the same for any two conversing,
separated as we were by fingerprint,
footfall, voice, and time served.

I joined in
with an elaboration
of what could be the last station,
a place in the searing glamour
of the stratosphere, its trembling stars
and charged auroras.

from
FEVER

(Dos Madres Press, 2019)

Premonition

Fallen grapes eaten beneath the vines' enclosure.
All those annoying twists and tangles.

Wiser not to dwell on *complexity*
but feast on regenerative imagination.
A drop of water on the lilypad
alerts me to possibilities in the field.

What enthralling methods I shall devise
to keep the spider from the shoe
and the bee from supping with me
when viands are on the table.

Fusion

The guild does not accept raw musings. Come back, then,
when there is fusion, the more cooked, the more meritorious;
the more invigorating, the more bound to linger on the cusp
of delightful. The stove ignites, four ticks toward a flame,
a light to guide the fire home.

Cleave to a plan. Weld it to a whole.

Fierce

How does vivid pain suddenly disappear
so that the wonder becomes
that the invasion ever took place at all. Yet
the memory of it lingers as potent as the original pain
which, having disappeared, allows a relief as boundless
as asperitas clouds dipping down like mounds of ice cream
overturned from their cones, cool and distant but part
of the expanse.

With pain gone, such lightness of body slightly mitigates
the mind still embroiled
in dark meanderings, hard to simplify.

That is the meaning of asperitas: uneven, rough, difficult,
fierce.

A Sporting Chance

There is a place for things not understood,
a storage chamber creaking with age.
Oil only when comprehension is complete
after many precious ponderings.

The chamber contains mounds
of cautionary advice, fine spices meant to keep
stupid happenstance at bay.

I say the marketplace could be kinder.
It likes to thwart
indulgence and any sly merriment.

It is said a plunge pool is exhilarating. First the plunge,
then the exhilaration.

Only keep at it—whatever the action, whatever the return.
If not, a fog of loss will drift to the borders of the page.

I'm not listening.
Yet there is a refrain.

Frisson

A thunderstorm is unfolding. She sees it coming, hears
the tornado's gripe, wants to kill it. Then the sun auditions
and so does the hawk, each its own act, each punctuating
like a leading man. There's a shiver of excitement.

She walks home in the chromium mist.

Together and Getting On With It

This is the twenty-fifth anniversary
of our narrative.
Thanks to luck and artful practice,
we were able to find a favorite
and be one.

I cannot dwell on every moment
of this existence. Happy to leave
that to Stevie Smith,
her daily entries into the gloomy
retrosphere.

Our own silliness and profundities
reveal that of late, and in retrospect,
all has been well.
Height and weight unchanged. We look good.

We can foil any tears which otherwise
would drown a misery,
for the underlying secret
is that only harmony will keep at bay
the cataract
cascading over the precipice.

Reconnaissance

From the bay window's embrasure
she looked out at all that drama,
feeling sentimental about the expanse,
the night sky spilling
as through a slotted spoon, its starry gems.

No, that is not how it was.
From the bay window's embrasure
it came to her that the only way to live
is without desperation,
to live as a fearless interloper
into the fields beyond.

Then move stealthily. One never knows
what joy is waiting, and how to scramble
toward it by clever means.

All those breaks of day, all those side trips
on the way to the next coast,
all those intricate weavings, those evolving
secret incantations,
all as yet unsimplified and under investigation.

Evidence gathered
from the bay window's embrasure
indicates that what her intellect doesn't know
about desire, it will find in distant notebooks,
those many indelible gushings,
such a private splendor of emotions
from voices in the universe, yielding
this page, dear friend, whoever you are.

Fortune's Always Hiding

I can riff on a word
but forget yesterday's conversation.

That is a ridiculous quandary—
eloquence lost
against the drift of delectable indolence.

Conversely,
take this lotus. It affirms
perpetual motion,
the eternal longing to rise
and search for placement,
even immortality.

Ready

The foundation
gladly takes mortar laid on with a trowel.
I can't clarify who claims the design
for there is no drafting, only hymns and speech
to render everything I hear and see.

A plinth of white concrete is the bedrock.
A divine work of muted mystique,
a chastened installment in the building
of the spire.

My own temple until the dew settles,
and in that, a hint
of heaven.

A moment, please, for the pulse to quicken.

I saw the pink cloud journeying, and heard a whistle.

Flowers in a Vase

She resists the amber starburst of potions and elixirs
which is precisely why the pangs began in the first place.

Hail comes as a respite, small icy pellets on grass,
and just at that velvet interlude she invites him in,
envisioning a litany of daffodils already risen
as if March were April, and February, March.

Her aqua slippers
are ready at the door in perfect exactitude,
a symbol of the little green plot
which the fountain cannot reach
except by manipulation.

Stick with me, I'm the fella you came in with,
says the guy to the doll.

His choice bouquet stays the night.
Bright blue flowers fade to a nether-white
in a nether-world where secrets are forbidden by law.

Few Distortions

The sea meant everything to her imagination.
Immensity. Purpose. New calculations
with every curlicue of seaspray. Unstoppable spigot.

She looks to the sea for reflection.
No shame in solitude.

May the ship swim well! cried Captain Bligh.

She falls in with the raptors
making their way through clouds and traffic.

The Healing Song of Standing Rock

My heart is red and sweet, and I know it is sweet because
whatever passes near me puts out its tongue to me....
—Sitting Bull

Not war chant, not the painted rail,
not the calling day
can obstruct the gradient climb
to the plateau
where, because they can see color, angels
congregate to offer pleasantries and advice
often followed by musical notes.

The heartbreak
of their honest song
takes us higher and higher.

Moon of the drying grass.
Moon of the falling leaves.
Moon of the strong cold.
Moon of the red blooming lilies.
Early in the moon of popping trees.
Moon when the white geese shed their feathers.

On the Mend

After many rickety launches,
what things are knowable
I want to know.

I heard eleven bells
after which I dreamed a lucid dream,
foiling the nightmare
which dared to invade.
The dream's hero nodded
in my direction,
toward the brimming orchard's
lucky boughs.

Having plucked and eaten
the hours,
we retreated, each to our home,
his over the rooftops (choice clouds
at the outermost pinnacle
of the mirage of mountains), and mine
toward the sea.
Look at all that shimmering!

These obsessions get me through the night.
After gripes are dismissed from mind,
the quarry yields.

Sparring with a Reflection

The darts have been flung.
Effects are in the mercurial mirror,
each mood suspended there
until reckoned with by a shrug.

Now and then the nectar of memory
reaches the magic place
mentioned in the contract,
and observations tallied
are put to use.

Still there, the silken hair,
lips fairly represented.
Fine lashes resting lightly on the lid
secure a place in the annals
of the appealing eye.
Yet the mirror's reflection, casting shadows
cautions, *Let's be amigos*
and keep small-talk to a minimum.

The Zen way to keep the dark at bay
is to keep the inner space a sanctuary
before the next scheduled bout
before the mirror.

Chronicles of an Antediluvian

Oh those lingering miseries,
days replete with assignations, aspersions,
and beautiful rage.

Fifty columns, one for each year of investigation.
The rapture of being alive.

Or five columns, each representing
a decade, an Appian Way of cypresses
leading to the longing for ever more
cypresses on the hillside.

A few morning stars and evening stars,
a few monsoons. The late train loads
and is presumed to be heading
toward Rome through periods
of stopping and somnolence.

Then the engine picks up speed
and races toward the thunderhead.
The close-up reveals a network of citizens
repeating, *Quo vadis?*

I manage to say I was away
and this is where I've landed.

The alarms of the past
(signaled through a conch shell
over the aqueduct)
have been questioned and quelled.
Now my heart trades in little satisfactions.

One Stellar Eve

One stellar eve we walked out to find
a cold dew had already descended in preparation
for a killing frost, the one that beheads
the still laboring lilies.

What we know about labor is equally disarming—
the kind of labor which takes you
by the hand to the terminus
unless you plead for an extension
or have the kind of temperament which allows
the shoulders to relax
during cloud-watching exercises,
in itself a distinctive endeavor, though
too solitary an act to be officially endearing.

To love the clouds is to inhabit them,
with a certain discretion, of course.
Less fear and more inclination
takes one into the stratosphere.

Happy are we who get to roam there.

Existential Fever

When the long tyranny of school
is over, and the lessons' words
which froze in the northern air as they were uttered
become audible when thawed,
we leave the halls
as salmon leave their cover
and face the rapids configuring
one after another.

When through the night
the train whistles undaunted
down the countryside, skirting
the reflecting pool's edge,
one can still see narcissus
and hedges hiding the red fox,
redder on the run.

When will we be done
after all these years of study, sweat
and whetted appetite
with chasing after Beauty's thrall?

A small garden's walled perimeter
is where instruction ends in a shower
of conceptions,
and the lessons' words
which froze in the northern air as they were uttered
now call and coax as stem to flower.

Clarity

Open, world, in all your disguises—

though there is no easy way from the earth to the stars. Hark
back to the dream and dream in praise of optimism. Wait!
It's coming now, like a comet which has been longing
to show off its brimming head. Petition the sky for a favorable
glimpse, and wipe any tears of joy with a natural detergent.
All the centuries passing by, and she abides in this one.
A gift not to be taken lightly, especially when eyesight
is still so keen and the looming azure and adelaide-yellow
asperitas clouds are right before her.

X

Today's drama of significance is all of one color.
The lecturer sticks to the topic, which is x. Shelter
can be found in x in palest blue. Among the sharps
and monochromes, x is untouchable.
Fond memory also has a part to play, for to hold memory
that long
is the cru x of happiness.
Only believe in ebb and flow as the factors
which promulgate each new vision, for visions
are the impetus for removing the bathrobe, dressing,
venturing out when the hours seem friendly.

It is never regrettable to be without an errand.

From What Just Was

I hesitate to reminisce, fearing
faulty interpretation.
That is my smug design
(tinged with resignation)
to keep secure the beauty
of a simpler time
which served as a cure for my malady.

It is enough that the sharp night
and crude dawn are waiting
with their own messages, mostly unkind,
calling back the melancholy
which was thought to be chronicled and purged.

There may sometimes be a nod
from someone dear
who wants to hear a dreary bit
about how sharper than cold
was the fever.

That is why I plead selective memory
when pressed to recount my history.
I taught myself how not to pitch
a woeful dirge to others
who have their own to listen to.

Mail lingers in the box
and the postman sneers with each deposit.
I shall write him a little note. *Please
leave today's stash at another mooring.
I am busy navigating
from what just was to what is just about to be.*

Atelier

He is dappling the copper
with a peening hammer
and folding back the wing-tips.

I am pulverizing
phrases until the pith is refined
and resonates.

We take these tasks seriously
to keep the work sparking
until daybreak calls
and we make our entry
into the morning wilds.

Though our wares may fall into the oubliette,
it is our privileged duty just to be,
and to speak our languages trippingly.

Walk Swim Fly

I buy a ticket and reserve the change.
On voyages to places significant
only to me, the drama of each move
is sharp and tightly staged.

If theatre tells us anything,
it's that conventional rules do not apply,
allowing the virtual traveler to bask in possibility
without so much as a bob and weave.

I bought my ticket to discover and inhabit
all the gradient hills earth is hiding.

The image of the next fresh morning
in a different place
rests easily against my isolate heart.
That is optimism and I desire it,
desire passage to sands alongside the sea,
its vibrancy home to me.

Anywhere but the dreary here,
the common city spewing dust and oxides,
a pessimist's delirium dictating
that to allow one atrocity on stage
is to plan for the next one.

I am in the arena
with a ticket valid for any given day.
Walk, swim, fly.

Strength

Strength has returned to ribs, wrist, fingers.
I can now deal a blow, if required.
Nothing emotional.
I can easily survive the slightest current of wind
or tide, and lift a steel ingot.

I am happy to inform opposing parties
that I will be on the lookout for any ploys to disrupt
or change my lucky circumstances.

Do not seek me indoors where a rise
in body temperature might stealthily evolve.

I prefer the valley where sheep in sunlight
feed on fiddleheads and sprigs of purslane.

I am sturdy, sharp.
No ailing, no convalescence.

Been Searchin'

To find a footing is to construct
a plan, one that reverberates
beyond the garden grid.

Until then, how are the intervals filled
between flower and fruit?

Sun's singeing impact, rain's moody
dispersal, stars brandishing their tidy glory,
ply their influence
for any one of us just living the hours.

True to the nature of the game
and worth all the universe,
we gain composure,
men of flesh and fiber cooling our daily fever,
not expecting never to die,
only to manage what we've put by.

Little Philosopher II

Every hour the sky changes.
As one looks up for the show
it's so easy to trip on the pavement.

Then the day arranges itself
without a word from anyone else.
Better, as moments are dealt, to follow
one's own pattern according
to the law of the day.

Say that law can be tweaked
to allow some prankish play.
As Mallarmé rolls the dice,
one can bet a life or a shirt
that a prize is on tap for just flirting
with the game, not inanely
squandering it.

Gathering While I May

I was a botanist once
in my reckless youth.
Fields of wildflowers
empowered me.
I fell for color patterns
and stalks of showy inflorescence
vaulting higher and higher.

I never took lightly the look
of nodding sweetpea,
white-fringed orchid,
winter-cress yellowing a meadow,
stonecrop's mossy mat of starry flowers.

That phase, my youthful
joyous jealousy of all that beauty
only led to later jealous passions,
the hidden away, every-day inner
workings of impulse and innuendo
copious as fleurs-de-lys of the field,
each year differently revealed
and sometimes ponderous.

An existential fever dictates
the mood of each rhapsodic hour.
This bud that bears today
will join tomorrow's
shockingly succinct
gatherings of the garden of the mind.

Ease

So easy to be receptive when a fever mellows,
especially when magnolia is in its first phase of bloom
on a purposeful day, emitting perfumes for everyone's
benefit and pleasure.

On the hillside, elemental forms are heard murmuring.
A lizard in natural surroundings is a kindred species,
its prissy coat and slick gait.

I have been given a rare taste of contentment infused
with energy because a sweet May breeze—more like
a trade wind—has engendered the prettiest bird calls,
the pretty birds in chorus calling.

Tranquil noon has passed. Evening presents with a rash
of yellow irises primping here and there through the mead's
tall grasses.

A finger pressing on the neck's trigger point relaxes
the melancholy aches which usually accompany
my interpretation of the hours.
Now all is fine as fine can be.

from
EQUAL PARTS SUN AND SHADE:
AN ALMANAC OF PRECARIOUS DAYS

(Aldrich Press, 2017)

Brevity: A Prologue

True and significant in ways
I am about to tell,
this summary of passing days
is just enough to feather-fill a pillow.

If a bit of ale is desired
before the telling, go ahead
down the leafy path for a draught.

Libation and listening are balm for the soul
and so are asides
for they may tickle more than the story, as when
six turkeys pass through the barley field, peck
and pass by, then on into the shady brambles
(where A has consented to accompany B
for a look at the moon).

The forecaster's finicky permission
(to confide this chronicle of passing days)
has been granted.
I have tested each nuance for its relevance,
going as fast
as sprouting grain will rise.

As for truth without garnish, at last
it appears—
odd meta-lingo but the best-laid
line-to-line configuration.

Form and I have so many times argued
and engaged in combat.

Sufficiently armed,
I hone my tools—
transit and gauge

without which

I would miss the sky most.
The oceans, too, but the sky
most,
open to measurement
and a poet's brief raptures.

Feasibility Study

I have surveyed my habitat
from cloistered feet to finger bone.
The findings: remarkably solid,
like cherubs on a frieze.

Using my expertise as master
surveyor of whatever abounds,
I measure farm and field
through four-dimensional Euclidian space
and linger with livestock
in the warm afternoon.
We snort, graze, stretch forth
a leg and lick, bleat, roam, lie down
where shoots escape and push.

It is a simple scene,
appreciated most
by those who have an obsession
with specifications and alterations.

At the farmhouse, bread breaks,
eaters swoon, moments prolonged
by *ohs* and *ahs.*

Drowsy by evening,
surveyors call each other awake.
We scrape our boots
covered in clay
because tonight the architect is coming
to verify how well we have spent our days
and marked our byways.

From the Wings

The angel Cassiel contemplates his immortality.
—*Wings of Desire,* 1987

That's what makes me clumsy—
the absence of pleasure.

Then how should I live? Maybe
that's not the question.
How should I think!

How should I inhabit the house
inside a house
where I long to suspect
and not to know,
for knowing is a dread
and a discomfort.

Best is the short day.
But what if time were the illness,
the thought that someday the one who I am
will no longer be the one I am,

the one who used to say *ah, oh*—
for that was the pleasure.

Prisoner's Lament

Who was I once
and why have I been corrupted?

The mind of an analyst cannot discover
who I once was,
what caused my stride to break
while on leave at the prison yard,
how I had to disappear
until someone from Amnesty came to ask,
Where?

Open the guarded doors, I beg,
to where the fronds are a frilly green in the glade,
sky a pampering reprieve.

There flies the weightless crane,
feathered still and negotiating with the winds
about how best to go the vital distance.

Volume

Seemingly
a tranquil day across the region,
a few cooler spots toward Canada
where pilings rise up from the sea
to join the superstructure.

Pragmatic
(in itself a daunting exercise)
as I cross the bridge,
yet sentimental
at the last light of day,
my way is underscored by one
reductive question.
What should I listen for?

I have not received hints
from any collective.

Luckily
this is not Vancouver's rainy season
so I chance to stop
where two park benches meet
to study the pharmacology of leaves.
Sequestered in my briefcase are rules to follow
while investigating such phenomena
if a searchlight is not available.

I hear the trees opining,
Accept plenitude. Reject platitude.
Though bromides have long been a favorite fizz,
this advice enables me
to get some swagger back.

Against Breakage

Little triumphs arrive
just in time to save
the frame
and keep the rest from shattering.

Whatever the business at hand,
may it be dutifully performed.
This will clear the landscape
so that all pieces fit without heartache
within the enchanted border.

Wrapped Up

Concealed in a newspaper
like fish and chips,
oily and sometimes with vinegar,
are stories that journalists want readers
to feast on.

There are the emotive underpinnings
of pity in reports of atrocities
and annihilations.
None of us want to live
that dystopian existence
which reams the heart in two....

Was there ever Utopia? Maybe
for a satisfied child.
For the rest of us pilgrims,
not for long at any rate.

Are you saying that Art
is the savior because it soothes,
perplexes, and takes us beyond
the mirror's dark backing?

Yes, for then the mind is at full speed
without the body's need to hurry.

Clairvoyance

*If I eat a pink cake, the taste of it is pink; the light sugary perfume,
the oiliness of the butter crème are the pink. Thus I eat the pink as
I see the sugary.*
                                    —Jean-Paul Sartre

Second sight brightens day
without a counterpunch, relinquishing
the present tense
in favor of the future
which isn't too rotund these days,
prospects (of marriage) wearing thin
so that one must be wary
in the maelstrom
to catch any over-spilling clouds
of wedding rice,
the spice of the best love-letters
ever written
with the exception of Emily's
letters to the world
that never wrote to her.

The eddying currents of conflicting
tides may override the odds
that the prospects (of marriage) will fatten,
that the wedding cake will be pink
and sugary,
the bouquet fraught with diamonds
caught beneath a sky of spent stars,
the parting day
accepted and admired.

Expectation

This is the right moment
to fashion a future,
a future such as the one that goes back
to when I said *yes*—

and I kept to that affirmative
gladly, wholeheartedly,
attuned to its measures.

If there is such an enemy as *once,*
or a pronouncement such as *forever,*
I leave them both behind.

This is the right moment
to ward off any disturbance
in the atmosphere
and give a quick, quirky knock at the door.

Turmoil

When it comes
to delicate and precise steps,
I get in my own way
like a Valiant misfiring
at cylinder number three.
Once that sparkplug
is replaced,
things will be all right
for a while.

The rainy season
will show my talent
for persevering
in muddy terrain.

Limbering up
will come quickly enough,
sun working its angles
to absorb any infiltrating
mists and puddles,
leaving sky white with possibility.

Still, answers are needed.
A quotes B
provoking further uncertainty.

A: The river is black today.
B: There are no sightings.

The Lifesaving Properties of Solitude

Left with imagination's wounds,
I let fly over the Baltic a dream
of twenty petrels so tight in flight
they tweaked the Polish border
where there is no glamour
but some notable ancestry.

I extracted from my storehouse
ten-pound peals of laughter
for general buoyancy,
for the days are long and need to be infused
with perks
wherever one may find them.

I waited through March's two waning moons,
thinking the planets
might conjoin and there would come others
with whom to break bread
if only for general displacement of melancholy
and to shake up any seraphs on pre-dawn standby.

Epistle

There was no intrusion of menacing
light, no design to foil passage
down the usual byways,
just some violet markings
across the sky, foretelling
inclement weather.

No rain fell in silver sheets,
just some dew
upon the branches
where a few buds swelled.

No buds opened,
just bougainvillea burgeoning
within the appointed cycle,
no tolerance
for false starts or perjury.

So were the intervals filled
between flower and fruit,
dispersed and handed down,
relevant to the natural order as a pulse
at wrist or carotid artery.

I Love a Little Folly

I love the spontaneity of make-believe.
It culminates every time in rhapsodic
illusion

as when autumn leaves seen rustling
at the door
are really cellophane strips, a paper buttress
against drafts of chill air
desiring a fleeting respite there.

Other mirages
have yet to be investigated, but right now
the comfort provided by he who sits
beside me on this bench is precious,
we two watching a frieze in the making
of autumn hills, and commiserating
as trees cry out
for sartorial relief from solitary
green
in favor of flamboyance.

Here we have convened
for general discussion and invigoration.
All this without the committee's approval,
proving that enchantment is never far away.

Right Now

Why not accept this moment
for how swiftly
it enveloped my senses,
unfolding in a pattern so natural
that I felt it to be a moment of beauty,
second in impact only
to a moment of sorrow—

until its marvelous extinction,
its appearance in another guise—
this one carrying a portent
of some kind of achievement.

Why not believe as much in portent
as in moonlight,
as much in the temporal as in the eternal seconds
during which raindrops still quiver.

Beauty Revisited

The cup is filled to brimming
and that is all the cup
will hold of useful content.

When night descends
with orders
to listen and take dictation,

raise to lips
another cup, as if it's tea—
still simmering.

Humility

It is so right, so fitting
that all my zeroes
add up to nothing lost,
and being round, can speed
to new territories in one easy roll.

On these voyages
I ask, *Where is the train station, citizen?*
or *Where is the war?*
for there is always a war going on someplace.
There is always an enemy
to thwart the elements.

Yet I feel no lingering regret
or doubt about destiny,
holding to the notion that the gods of sustenance
will assure that all endeavors
maintain their fruitfulness,
adding up to nothing lost.

Company

We sailed at dawn.
Pre-arrangement was made
with the river king
that shafts of pearly light would fall,
mists lift,
banks conduce to a perfumery
of jewelweed and gentian.

All of yesterday's debris,
branches and the shiny scales of bream
were to be given up by morning tide.

In this promising tableau
we saw an eagle rising.
It was the vernal equinox,
and other aspirants, too,
noticed eagles on a course.
That was the phase
at which the conversation began.

It was verified that by looking
over the water from the stern's vantage point
to portions of patterned sky,
one could discover
where such wings are coming from
and where they are off to.

Sentinel

Astonishment comes naturally.

It is my rule
to uncover what is really there,
my gift
to find evidence overlooked,
my thrill
to crystallize this moment's
enigma.

Skin of Mother's cheek
a petal so astonishing
that to touch it
is better than grieving.

Purpose

for Mark

The hand that makes the bread
cuts the bread.

No pain is felt by either,
just the sweet pangs heard
of serration.

The knife that cuts the bread
goes the way of resting cutlery.
It had a purpose, nothing as gallant

as a thrumming
on the crust to test doneness
by the same hand
that dithers on the harpstrings.

Daily Bread and Cheese

Who standing here is not ready
for the brutal mix
of another day, hoping
there will surely be the kindness
of reward ahead
in the form of sustenance,
such as the taking of daily bread
and cheese, along with a morsel
of something raw and nutty,
so that after thirty-one obsidian nights
the wall will become a page,
a page encountered many times before
but which now seems quite new.

Cruising

Nothing in tow, nothing
to trade. Free
as a popsicle from its stick,
eaten and enjoyed.

Sun sinks to a low
here in Key West, though
lower still in Bimini.

One can fish almost to dawn
now that tasks are done
and reverie is at last at hand.

No anchor, no prongs, no bait
because the fish come to you
in all their silvery goodness.

On the Move

It is a corruption of time
to cry over the garden wall
that summer's green
has ended in Manhattan's
little parks
and the sun that suited so well
will now burnish
other islands
being particularly fond of The Virgins,
their waters so beguiling
that any sentient being
would long to follow
as birds-of-paradise
follow the ripening feast
from tree to tree.

Sixth of April

Vernal pools are singing—
frogs in their antic heyday,
heads over flying heels,
their awakening commotion,
oxygen combustion,
spent silliness by the hour.

As for me, ten minutes to five,
and still no wish to swim beyond
the beckoning buoys.

Frogs, I love
your imperfections, especially
your speech impediments, specifically
the diphthongs.
Your atonal, irritating timbre announces
your capricious disregard for anyone
standing watch at the pool,
trying to get your drift.

Infinity: An Epilogue

The slickest caper
is to live in the world
between safety and danger.

Should thirst persist there,
believe it to be only a trivial thirst
which should not trouble love.

Just in case,
there is a pillbox on the divan
to indicate
a glass of water may be near.

The children walked through the little gate
and I ran to meet them in the garden,
rose campion's silver leafage
graven by teardrops.

Remember how I poured
milk before water,
creamed and plenty of it
till you little ones swooned?

The glass, the garden, the hour.

Remember how we loved
to watch two waxwings safe
in their twiggy bower,
how they remained when we pursued,
how they loved our company
and, in the heart of morning, how we loved
to watch them drinking from our basin?

If love will delay dying,
love anything.

from
MINDING THE SPECTRUM'S BUSINESS

(FutureCycle Press, 2015)

Charting the Expanse

A spare room, though it be sparse,
is the handout I crave,
an extra room which cannot be shared—
for the one within
is given it as a favor
and place to rest
from discomfort or cold.

Do not mind living
in the extra room,
for it is only a spare bone
and a respite.

Looking through binoculars
at the hawk in a tree
one can see the day is all about finding
a spare meal which, when digested,
enables a thing to better fly.
Restlessness is the only price to pay,

paving the way for the rest of the saga
and the eye that goes with it.

The flinty couch is mine alone
and so is the shivering white lunarscape
out the window.

An Eye at the Key-Hole

His eye at the key-hole, this is what the poet sees...
an unending spiral....
     —Cocteau, *The Blood of a Poet*

Scent of perfume
when there is none,
just the atomizer.
Windows open to a breeze
what little there is
as the pendulum swings.

There should not be pepper in the little mill,
but there is some.
This is the portrayal through the key-hole
of a poet's room.
It wants to be painted
after the rubble is cleared
leaving titanium-white walls
and a small—let's say meditation bench—
for authenticity.

A daily peek through the key-hole
is music for the spirit,
an unending spiral
which lends composure to battle,
at least while the grass is still greening
which is for only a moment in time,
a cunning move
to claim space, every inch of ground
covered
except where deer have trod in the night.

All Rise

It is worth descending
if only to rise.
That is what they tell me
when I rise
from a bed of water, a waterbed so buoyant
it is great to be on land again.

Worth the weight
when I rise
as a balloon released
from the breakfast nook
having buttered and jammed
and worked the grapefruit segments
counter-clockwise.

A luminous break
from the fast held overnight
with no great suffering,
breaking from a sleep
wherein I floated without assistance
under a baby blue, arched ceiling
of sapphire boats.

Smartly garbed, first in thought I rise,
then in deed
and prepare to enter the workplace.

There, they all rise
to greet me
for I have been gone so long.

Very Rich Hours

Now to drop with a thud silver linings
and settle for the familiar.

A whistle is heard from high
in a poplar,
a satisfied, yes, a smug
little mockingbird calls
and had I not wandered out at noon
in the field beyond this solitary acre,
I'd have listened to its opinion.

I'd have supervised
as the four-footeds run for cover where I roam
to hyperventilate deep in their holes.
(What are you renegades up to?)

Yes, skunks and coons
do visit this spindly acre at night.
I have been able to notice
a few fast-moving rumps
fleeing by moonlight.
But when my little world
in Spring is greening,
they do not dare appear
because I bare my teeth
and wave some stinging nettle.

I mind this property without a telescope.
Each task, well done,
can be set aside in all tranquility.

Self-scrutiny remains a fever.

Complacencies to Live By

Western thought proposes
that the spirit
journey toward its given end,
but make it a splendid, the best ever
end, one with a surplus of surprises
as when the boardwalk scale
for fifty cents announces
Your weight and your destiny.

The best destiny ever:
intimacy with light
and shadow,
each step of the way recorded
with an ear
for the discordant,
an eye for the disconcerting.

And toward journey's end,
who would not miss the sky most,
its scarlet twists and pink brocades,
an embroidered sky
to keep the self in earthly thrall
even through thunder.

Momentum

As leaves dress a tree,
so do I fix and fuss,
so do I trim.

As bark encircles ring,
so do I envy protection,
so do I limit and exclude.

Sun torques
to my lodge
at the crux of noon.

Letter E catches beams
while the rest of the weathervane
poses, does not turn
though the heron is hot to fly toward W
and all along Cape Flattery.

Constructing reveries of this sort
is helpful to the heart, though most illusions
gather momentum
on their own,
just windforce, sheer bravado,
hum of voices,
submission,
jangling of the mind's keys
between stations.

Existentialism 101

Definition of a soul? Anyone?
And where found?
Somewhere deeply buried.

A clean white placard, a cloth,
most likely cotton, most likely
starched.

The ear calls the soul,
calls the starched cotton
to arms.
Something is up.

Something the opposite
of a placid mooring.

Anyone? Offer a dollop
of pudding,
a real taste of the concept
that is soul,
which concept arrives around age three,
the age at which one learns
to keep a lid on any moral or spiritual
underpinnings,
while keeping pristine
the starched white cotton pinafore.

About Beauty

About Beauty and its revelations
(which Memory is keen to keep
as if a bird ushered in
actually fluttered),

we are poised to rediscover
a flock of willets rising from the mangroves,
daffy clouds high above,
a promise of south wind;

poised to remember
that onyx has a place on the palette,
that incoming waves are made of it.

Our dwelling's downward from Hull Bay
where garden and sea suffice as World.

We are the couple on the littoral far off.
(He takes her picture.
She fluffs her skirt.)

Softly Through the Woods

On the forest floor
a Pandora's box of leeks and quirky ramps
yielding
as moss to a footfall.

Softly through the woods
footfalls scatter swallows and pipits
(their cries of lamentation)
from woodland chasms.

This is how Memory operates—
a drift
of feathers, a thought taking wing
as it did when original—
the first thought about Love,
the now fabulist memories
upon which to build a bed of grass and nettles.

Deep Attachment

Evening is nigh,
horizon sedate.
It's time we began to bicker.

Your raptor's beak looks ready
as a sharpened point to penetrate.

Tonight we will argue love, lust,
and jurisprudence.

You suggest rules of order
but I am a fountain
of extraneous perplexities
and melancholy redundancies.

I preen and posture, you uphold.
How I adore the precious exchange of minutes,
taut and slowly pulsing.

We play out to the end, a civil court.
There is no reliquary
of bent knives, spent forks.
With my permission you advance
to kiss the wounded breath of love
before going in for the kill.

Manners at the Round Table

That is why
there was so little known then
about courtesy, that rarity,
though not as rare as chivalry,
that relic
of the age of Sherwood Forest's band
of sweetheart thieves.

That is, if by thieves,
one means grabbers of goods
or affections.
That is, if by recipients of the bounty
one means those to whom the grabbed goods
are presented.

I steal for you because it's empowering.
I cook plucked goose for you
because I love you,
and on the hit list
is the helmeted guinea fowl.

Hold the sweetbreads! Buff the armor!

Flimsy vows to protect and tend
are made in a frenzied state
in which emotions eddy, a pond
ducks have dipped into
and what we wouldn't give for a little down.

Striking a Chord Across Time

In the beginning, love was a plainsong
heard simply as wind
rushing through hectares of tall grass.

As only love can witness,
the grass yielding
engendered the next chord.

That chord investigated
the crucial—
how love deepens.

There was also a time when rain
was fresh rain
for flower and basin.

One cannot ask *why*
about love or a term of apprenticeship,
only retrieve and remember.

Light Lesson

The Upper Side of the Sky, 1944 oil on canvas
—Kay Sage, Surrealist

The shadow of my house
falls on the lawn.
It looks like the shadow
of a barn
but it is the shadow of my house falling
on the lawn.
There never was a barn
and this can be proven by the shadow
of a chimney on the roof
of the house's shadow.

Furthermore,
the upper lode of sky
has spun a shadow
between the door and kitchen floor
but it's not my checkered floor,
it's not my kitchen from which a yellow curtain flutters,
though the idea of a yellow curtain fluttering
takes hold like a stark new city of implausibles
serving to minimize
the cozy shadow of my house.

It's clear that light (so loud when near,
ear stands in for eye)
obliterates obscurity
as light is meant to do;
and clear
(footfalls on the checkered floor,
the curtain waving near)
that though home is where the light is—
intimacy with shadow
makes one free to walk the world.

Swizzle Stick

Waves have lost their fizz,
all being as it should on a dull night
in Atlantic City after the storm
when gambling on anything
is of no use to the universe.

If one could siphon energy
from catastrophe,
harmony from ruin,
there would be left a rich little world
of dignity and sharp ideas.

As it stands now, the warning
is to stay safe because clusters of dignitaries
from the Venus Casino
are arriving
to foment their theories about winning
and replenishing,
but those theories are ignorant of strategy,
airy foam on a wave,
wind moaning through the arcade.

Love Ever, Sam

Throughout the petty ambush
of bees among the daylilies
I read the letters
of Samuel Beckett.

Sam to Tom McGreevy:
I like that crouching, brooding quality in Keats.

Dublin is lovely with no trains and buses,
the hills and sea seem to have crept nearer.

The letters state every indolence
and indiscretion,
excel at sympathy and empathy,
now and then take sides.

I read while waiting
on the green, awash with daylilies.
It is a prescient morning in May
where beyond the courthouse Corinthians
murmurs a small choir of maples.

A juror, enlisted for impartiality,
is taking his oath to tell the truth
while another with potential
reads *The Tempest.*

Ariel to Prospero:
Hell is empty, and all the devils are here.

Sam to Tom McGreevy:
I would like to live in a perpetual September—
watch kites fly.

Love, ever.

A Vague Unease

Apprehension!
That is why the clock
faces the wall
or no clock at all.
Side-splitting laughter
would be a relief, or at least
a tender burst of sunlight
at some hour in the day,
preferably toward late afternoon.
Then by evening, oh, yes
a reprieve does come
with the layout for a simple supper,
a stick-to-the-bones confabulation.

Do not get me going—though a tangent
often serves to titillate
the original story line,
especially when delivery is replete with sighs
of either dissatisfaction
or satisfaction
as when ginkgo's lobed leaves fall,
pretty scalloped fans
underfoot.

Oh, yes, this is a vague unease
a mild complaint of unknown origin,
what is called idiopathic
and I never know what small gripe
will get it going,
a bee, for example, on the screen
or a weakness in the floor.

Pes Anserine

That's what hurts.
The conjoined tendons of the pes anserine
splayed out as a goosefoot
and swelling at the inside knee.
Do not cry out until it worsens
at pre-dawn and our ordinary walk
to the river becomes a dumb notion.
We do not need to see
those rampant Canada geese
and their copies. Harpies all.

Across the river, percussing
like a complaining knee,
there are crashings at the coal plant, a sifting
and dumping of minerals, a grimy waste
in toxic plumes.

What befalls in the celestial commotion
of the pre-dawn universe
is more reminiscent of a hell filled
with repetitive signatures
like the knee's grum S.O.S.

Save Our Souls.
Be light and heavy.
Live and thrive.

Self Portrait with Sour Grapes

Lyric hardball
is to be played with reverence
in the mind's court,
a game of solitaire
with sonic underpinnings.

The court is limed. I play
within its boxes
until I am the only one left wondering,
What is the point
of rules that kill momentum?

Better to play on a sunless day
as eyes have no tolerance for strobe.
Brow should remain cool throughout.

The grayer the day, the higher the stakes
because darker, as later,
implies a boundless field.

Cunning moves are made
in the misty relevance of twilight,
one's own overcast moody empire.

In this realm there is no need for triumph
or fleeting reward,
just a small honorarium
for having forged the fiord
when light was loved
and it did not hurt to falter.

Attitude

This is in reference to the ache
that launched a thousand lies,
created furrows and arches
on this brow, this back.

I present to a panel of my peers
a case of misappropriation
of the truth
concerning certain well-rubbed drawings
on the wall of a cave,
especially that of a girl retrieving water
from a rivulet.

The truth is, I am she
and I was carrying the water in a pitcher
to my shelter a furlong away
and through the cornfield.

When the alphabet slipped from my lips
I set down the pitcher and with full composure
wrote six chapters of a story.
Every line was hyperbole
but that furthered my advantage
which was that no one represented on the cave wall
would listen, anyway
to these delights and scraps,
and that is how I wanted it,
so tired was I of one-dimensional company.

In the following year, however, I had much of import
to share concerning actual events
but calling two-dimensional company to attention
proved impossible so that the ache
escalated to aggravation,
creating furrows and arches
on this brow, this back.

Progress

Temporary as lamplight in early morning,
last night's longing
etherizes to a mist.

The particular becomes the common.
This is a useful construct,
similar to perfecting one's first language
before learning another.

To formulate new parameters by noon
requires stealth and strategy
but nothing comes.
A plan is needed
so one is chosen
from those in transit.

It is the plan to staunch the heart
by encapsulating in one furtive move
all sun motes in the watch area
and storing them in a pocket pouch
to dispense as needed.

There is nothing so satisfying as a resolution.

Sun and Water

There are enough spies in the land
to find, finagle, and deliver
the object of desire—
information,
just information.
May delivery come as neatly
as a thrice-folded napkin
under a fork
just to the left of the white plate.

What will I do with so many bits
of information?
Gather and store in the root cellar
until cohesive.
Scrutinize the profusion for any unwanteds.
Seems so easy.

There may come a time, however,
when all I need for sustenance
will be sun and water.

To the Heart's Architect

I sometimes dream of a larger...house...of only one room, a vast, rude,
substantial, primitive hall, without ceiling or plastering....
—Thoreau, *Walden*

Let shell become home
without lathe or eaves
so light source may reach each way round.

Avoid mishap through measurement.

Construct below frost line.
Eye angles.
Mark distance between egg and sun.
Plan to face the early red noons that knock.
Capture water fast-flowing from a stream
of icy fissures.

To lie undisturbed, as clam in clay,
forego the whitewashed wall.

If isolation seems radical,
omit roof
and change cube to rotunda.

This is the blueprint, my heart,
field notes to consider daily
before the butter is spread
and after the bread is eaten.

The Tribe that Hid from Man

And so today, nothing is in jeopardy.
Alleluia, at least, for that.

I grant myself permission to take repose
upon a bench which maintains its brilliance;
fountain just as white
and a bird sipping there.

I don't want to go beyond
these first hundred yards,
which will prove
no one dear has yet parted company,
and peace persists.

That the Kreen-Akrore, forced to broach modern times,
forfeited to prospectors, cattle-breeders
and enemies
their peaceful existence and original
primal territory,
only served to secure their demise and degradation.

Paul McCartney performed his version
of *Kreen-Akrore* on iTunes,
nothing but drumbeats and birdcalls
of the Brazilian rainforest,
also available as a cellphone ringtone.

Myself, I have always liked the rim:
a glass, a pond, a moon.
Safe there from din and clatter,
minding only the spectrum's business.

From the Tower

Zealous
to the point of commitment
about the lifesaving properties
of solitude
and hating the prying of the perplexed
into one's affairs,
every solitaire
can recognize another.

Please do not enquire
nor invite us to the roundtable.
We have our own finicky forum.

This is not solipsism,
but freedom to expand.
It is not wreckage, but admiration
for its parts.

Distractions are merely
points at which thought revives,
silver over chrome,

each solitaire polishing
an overtone.

Preparation

Bird in the garden seeks.

Worm of a screw embeds in its wood.

Hand arranges violets in a cup.

Rubble of a room
holds certificates of honor
as issued.
(All that leverage for one crowing Chanticleer.)

Say one wants to get to the bottom
of the gloom,

to fathom it,
not sink deeper;

to design a failsafe
for tricky maneuvers.

Final parameters not yet set
even as cold mountain air
encapsulates in channels of the down jacket
after evening vespers.

I have this to say about the headstone:
in my absence don't change a word
or pulverize the rhythm

and leave the lingering refrain to me.

Circumstantial Evidence

A paper curlicue
remains
of my contractual obligation to the moment.

What was there to fear when signing,
for the witnesses were the scope of day
and the hope at night of relief
from thunder.

All in all, the contract unveiled
few false positives
beyond those lodged early in my second
to third decade,
when living my life like I knew Everything—
was the hapless propellant.

Let's just say there is no wreckage
up to now.
There is only instant repair.

Be it resolved
that as a member of the universe
in good standing
whose atoms will here linger in perpetual residence,
I will henceforth investigate each healing poultice.

Therefore
welcome, once withering flowers
for (after bitterness)
it's time again to flourish.

The river has begun to flow in tempo
and (trickery of the eye)
through the green membrane
trees are leafing.
Now is felt the cosmic against the body,
known as euphoria.

Ocean Reporter

To dawdle is to find
a kind of ease,
no nitroglycerine
just a hard look at the mists
from here.

It is Saturday
and there will be shouting
children and crowds to bear,
chatter and shining fruit at market.

Shall we?
Leave now?

One more day before rising,
before you will say:

Do you like this terrarium
which has been prepared for you

filled as necessary—equal parts sun and water.

Lead with the left leg when rising
with the tide.
Launch like a trawler hefting its net.

Atlantic Salvor

Well, scholar, you must endure worse luck sometime,
or you will never make a good angler.
  —Walton, *The Compleat Angler*

A fine way to hold back woes
is to become, if not the compleat angler,
the compleat semi-screwed-up human engine,
ripe for analysis,
who with luck, with luck I say,
daily gets a little closer.

Just-in-time inventory:
four yellow rescue boats abreast
float when day is mellow
and in the shallows
scout blennies and butterfish,
finding the storehouse empty.

It is time to give evidence—
Sky, the enforcer;
Sand, the equalizer;
Mind, the henchman.

This is not about dying
but approaching,
not about scrubbing the hull
but letting weeds muster
because destruction grieves
the common sphere.

from
A STUDY OF EXTREMES IN SIX SUITES

(Cherry Grove Collections, 2012)

Ad Astra

When first I made my way
with the heart and speed of a plow
toward a beckoning summit,

I heard, at the pinnacle,
a sublime commotion.

I asked for a general melody
but the clamor persisted,
for at this spot
pursued by so many without a Sherpa,

there was too much
beauty.

I gave space on the delicate approach
to fellow climbers,
for it was the hell of boredom
that first prompted us to stir.

Now we are nearing the stars
in slow flotation,
guiltless,
as if left alone in a confectionary,
or ravished
by a breadth of roses
upon a breach of blue.

Earth's Cries Recorded in Space

What is heard is the shattering
of language
as by a cosmic blast, black holes
ripping stars apart;

The onslaught is steady,
reliable as the confluence of day
and night;

brightest in that night
when a doomed star bursts like an oration
in a riptide of roiling dust and vapor;

most grievous in that instant
when madding lingo splits the azimuth
in fiery temper,
the glowing remains of caustic arguments
lingering until lost in infinite density.

The redeeming apology,
yet to be recorded in space,
is abstracted in *The Tale of the Right Mind.*

What is now known
is that it is possible to draw nearer
by piercing flux and fold,
sending a cable to The Ace
or a poem to the universe

without fever—
as when Earth was young
and dawn innocently brightened.

Precarious

Though we bounce well,
how afraid we are
of falling.

Farmer Ooms,
have you any liniment?

*Arnica in a vellum wrap might do,
or the sap of your own oration.*

To hell with rhyme,
it's metaphysical.

The real
is the memory
of the night the millennium began,
venal and voluptuous.

We had earned a good place
in the world.
No money was made but all our labors
were sweetened with thanks.

Thanks for not expectorating,
thanks for not killing eagles or the ozone,
and thanks for not setting fires;
some of us would still like
to see California.

Farmer Ooms,
have you any libation?
We want to stifle vitriol,
which like an adder creeps,
which like a wounded psyche
seeks elixir
and never finds.

Farmer Ooms,
have you any hemlock?

Crisis

The drawers are filled with stuff, snuff, underwear, underwhat,
overfilled, slips, sachets, all too briefs, like a life
that has wanted to extend, a solid beam,
to the fullest.

If wanting means staying afloat on a lily pad
until the lily perfumes,
one can see the anguish. If hunger means pulling in
at the Full Belly farm stand on a snowy night
only to find there's no fare, one can see the folly.

There's an under-the-volcano in each of us;
we weep freely, let loose at the slightest.
If that fractious cat hadn't jumped into a dream
this morning, guess who
would still be hanging out with Morpheus?

Do not temper an ascetic's indiscretions
or reveal a recluse's hideout.
And don't
rearrange the furniture
while these thoughts are a braided brass knob,
vengeful and loaded.

Sustenance

A word is dead/ When it is said,/ Some say.
I say it just/ Begins to live/ That day.
—Emily Dickinson

Letters are scribed by steady hand,
each O a clean rondel.

The fell of the dot over *i*
the halo of the crossed *t*
the cleft *w*
welded, the mound of the *h*
to its loop aligned.
Now you have the *with.*

The *Brilliance* is in the other words,
linked and cruising.
We have heard these words
sometimes as four to six eggs
in a feather-lined cup of grass;
sometimes as the beating of butterfly wings,
a final susurrus
through the trees.

Sated Paperweight

Bubbles
in a glass globe
smoothly resist my touch.

I'm a rookie
about substance and bubbles
but for today's dissertation
on iridescent light
call on me.

This glass globe,
this lamp of many lumens
contains a brightness impelled to scatter

while papers wait
counterpoised,
compacted and compressed.
Through the round I see engraved:

Here lie sequestered
the thoughts that I've squandered

over hill, valley, glade
and citied orifice.

Penultimate Chapter

A phrase still clinging
as whelk to rock
before the diver plucks;

a sentence beached
amidst plankton and urchin
at neap tide's fancy.

Beneath the sea-grape
my plot evolves,
the conflict and the cause
entwined.

Never will I spin
a narrative
wielding the jeweled
and poisoned rapier
of a specious thought.

Interrogate me
until I admit

I know the ending.
It seduces
as a silver shoal in moonlight.
It piques a sequel,
a little bite of sugar cane
which restoreth the whole.

Spring Scat Song: An American in London

Letter home

Over the din of new grass growing
Ella sings the bed-sit blues.

We read *The Guardian*'s early news
over English breakfast, eggs
with gruel. By half-eleven we descend
at Wandsworth Station
to the Tube.

Soon we're out with the animals
to nibble and stub,
to roam midst the heather
across Hampstead Heath.

We startle lovers
(Is it easier to be the intruder,
or to be intruded upon?)
below a tree

under the weight of blossoms.
Whatever her name is, her hospitality
engenders appetite.

But we pay no attention to the coos
of a yellow afternoon;
they're all the same (I'm talking Tate),
those Burne-Jones eyes.

A Little Bit Shy

for Dominic Behan

What's it to anyone how and when
I prime my canvas or my pen.

The muse imparts,
What's not art
that sears the soul,
prunes the mettle!

If mural mirrors reality
it's a haunting show.

The muse is sly, alluring,
an enigma.
I listen for her footfalls
in a verdant field.

My hat drops into a pond
as she puts four ripe tomatoes
on a white woolen blanket.

Her green sequins
cast flecks of green, quivering light
on her corsage and my carnation.

What's it to anyone if she's easy or true.
When she raises her slip, flirty and slow,
I become so inclined to unbuckle her shoe.

Another Love Poem

Chocolate and grief
they say, are excellent companions.
So are bees and butter; how the bees
alight on the mound of it.

He said we are mismatched.
(It's a little late
for that determination.)

An inspired rebuttal was imminent
but twilight began to penetrate
and Venus took her place atop the moon.

When I think about how the sea
throbs for its moon at every tide,
I exult that our relationship
has been just short of heavenly,
all seraphim being equal.

As for the mismatch comment,
it was spoken on a sultry day
at Jones Beach
after I proved I could swim a mile.

Listen, I said,
when the wind gusts had died down
and the heron passed leisurely
over the blue bridge,
What could we want in tepid night
but expectation of morning.

So home and to bed.

What Comes of Embrace

We're arched, tuned. Imprudent in any light,
yes, but naked fortitude, mistaken ardor.
Invoke all gods. Touch is world.

Guarded first sip. Original sin. Meadow.
Valley. All verdant in the end. Emerald
everywhere. Centered whims, careless truths.
All equal. To bed with birdsong throughout.
Every possible melody.

We hold to the essential as to savory pie.
Honeyed asides. I'm you, teamed like Trinidad
and Tobago, swamp oak and saxifrage.
Coupled, and no lacerations anywhere.
No report of bad behavior. No alarms.

Till the hills' soft verges. Till the sun rounds
like a clementine. Love feared lost for a moment...
but is found again, the gods invoked,
the light auspicious for travel.
Not too far.

A sweet icing-over when she's born,
a wildness in serenity.
We pass cigars, then chocolate gold doubloons
and spring up, bright as dandelions
that have escaped the cutter.

Treasury

All the errant hellos we keep track of!

And having said hello,
how bound are we?
Connect with a look, a trim kiss
on pale cheek?
Linger on the *o*
just to size the other up a little?

Whether lost in the marketplace or marbled gallery
Hello
is just a lesson in a missionary's handbook.
It doesn't mean a thing when compared to
Farewell.

And having said hello
to a classroom of kids bright and primary
as tulips in a garden, crepe-paper petals rolled tight,
I put my shining example before the board.

I am no missionary!
How can I explain this to my mother?

She smoothed her lipstick on
with her little finger.

I looked out at tulips through slats
in the blinds.
Petals were blowing off in the wind.
I ran to immortalize their flaming colors
with a camera.
All that digging!
Not so much the colors, but their names
lost with them.

Mother
says, *Greet friend*
as flower—

with all the force of an Ave!

 ...but when they arrive
for a judicious lunch of soup and toast,
majolica bowls
are the only elaboration.

And having said hello,
I lingered on the *o!*

noticing his earringed ear,
their clothes in evening slouch,
a hint of celestial perfume,
their pale blue *Hi*
and errant *Hey.*

Lucky

The funny thing about a broken branch
is its penchant to hang askew
the whole season
while rabbits toil, cattails
bloom to bursting, and we mark time
as if there were still an energy unexploited,
a field yet undiscovered
in the heart's hinterland,
that semi-precious habitat
wherein lies love.

And love does lie
after its soft-hued beginning.

The funny thing about beginnings
is that, lacking history,
they seem momentarily crucial, like a Lenten resolve,
like an underground spring aspiring
before sediment intrudes.

The funny thing about intrusion
is that it shocks the solitary place
painstakingly reserved.

The odd truth about solitaires?
Not built for misery or primed to cry,
they welcome lucky circumstance
and choice events above the treetops.

Above the pines may butterflies arrive
in orange shower,
winging on a hint of magnetite
or spell of the flower.

Nearer

On the train at Ticonderoga

Not my voice, but the train
   whistling its familiar.
Not my sparks, but wheel and track glinting,
   at it again.
Not my spirit, but the engine's
   refinement.
Not my body, but flatcars
   clattering.
Not my life, but the impact.
Not my news, but the effect
   of message upon ear,
      distance between opposites.

Not my crossing, but the train
   minding its drag and scrape.

Wakened
by scalding color
(these autumn leaves really know how to say
goodbye),
by purple loosestrife's inflorescent spire,
I bite and eat the mountains
that pass,
drink the blue remembrance,
savor what's stark or stunning on the way,
and disembark,
nearer.

Runner Reaches Lake by Sunset

Strengthened clavicle and tapered
thighs intact,
feet a region,
I'm back,
running alone, alerted,
wind rising and falling,
weeds flying, stones
electrified.

Footfalls quicken with sunset
and I alone mark
the comforting cold and syncopation,
red fern's plumage at the turn,
long, untethered stride.

Sun fades in crimson cusp
upon arum's sheath and lily's spathe,
so dark the lake, a draught denied—
another test satisfied.

Chasing Butterflies

In a slurry of crystal and snow
she aces the downhill run
slick as an arctic seal or harp's glissando.

Preferring boneless drifts
to company,

she drops every care
for the infinite possibilities
of negative space

and over white mounds
disappears.

As there can be no pose
without a poseur,
we have only rumor
that she'll come home.
(*Mind how you go!*)

Why should she reunite
and why should she explain

the snow's cold *ohs*!

Power and Potion

What you're saying about power
and potion
hurts,
dark and red.
I'll drink music as medicine.
It tastes good.

There was a stunning fall
from aloft, a hard left.
A wrist bone shaped like a boat
is now two boats, awash
against the semi-lunar in the front row
of bones.
What a ticket!

Try to navigate a bath
in a claw-footed tub!
There's danger
in the thought
and in the porcelain arrangement.

A skiff on a mission, ready
for the great wave that will knock me out,
I doubt my outlook is as murky
as it seems.
Daily I lift
slightly upward
to renew polarity with a delicate sun.

Nightly I play my moody fantasia.
Strings moan. Percussions bring me
to a stinging high.

The Adaptive Foe

The foe, they said, is in my head
but I shall seek a third opinion.

The enemy, engrossed and hidden,
any time now
may reach the shore
without even a warning foghorn
against the hapless collision.

Why this crimson vessel is allowed
to operate—
though forces are counterpoised
to handle any spidery intrusion—
is answerable before the outspread lexicon
of labials and plosives
which chatter and converge at the floodgate
till the story's told.

Till then, I won't be clipped
at the starboard bow in the shroud of night,
nor will I waver on the other side
like a ficus fig in a corruption of branches.
En garde!

A Birder's Diary

When I was a hawk meditating upon a meal,
my restive *skree* could stiffen any prey.

Offspring, if I'd had them, would have *skreed*
their own
into the night
but the thought of more of me was no more
than a beat winging to a word.

When I was a finch feathering a career,
my skyward notes earned a few blown kisses,

aerial bliss for an upstart alto heart.
Any birder in the field
could spy me,
a blazing dart in the hinting sun.

When I was a lark aloft in the plenum,
my evensong sweetened every glass

for I learned my lyric midst the flowering rushes,
all the while
the chambers of my heart receiving.

Though one day's gloom
may leave its bready remnants,
by formula or feint
we all sing when soaring.

Litmus Test: The Work-Up

Why so excitable
in the midst of all that grey?

Some havoc in the frame
when red trees ignite
in pulverizing laser-light.

The sheer calamity of obstruction!

Reprieve denied;
the periscope has been activated.
Violet first,
then blue giving way to grey,

then grey to mist,
and mist to ether.

After ether,
a delirious, kaleidoscopic riot of positives,
a happy sequence of iambs.

I am.

The Force of May

Spring holds back because
I must not be led into green haven
where leaves and grasses would appall
and soft winds distress me.

Though I lean upon the May which anoints
black day with dew,
I must not encourage harmony or growth,
having sinned

against my equal,
until this hour greening
in pale space, my deracinated flower.

Drella

I saw Andy Warhol among the collectibles
at Radio City,
no mistaking the oversized glasses,
platinum hair,
that voice.

That was years after Valerie Solanas
shot him at Union Square, piercing
seven major organs,
lungs punctured like isinglass;

and now here he was,
part Dracula, part Cinderella,
looking good again,

steady
as a luge,
always at his canvas:
Brillo, Kellogg's, multicolored Marilyns,
a thousand cans of soup.

If not honesty, then what?

Delicates, aesthetes,
to arms before the snow flies!
Unleash some art!

Oh, it's beautiful!—
the velvet underground.

Two Jims and Some Distractions

On a green bough extending north
an oriole knits a pouch
tight as a sheath.

On evening reconnaissance beneath the elm
I discover
how like an undertaker
he tapes and primes his room.

A mosquito soon inquires;
crickets play the drumroll
as I smack it into oblivion.

On the lawn there are chairs
separated from their table.
The oriole haggles with his twine.

Mourners
clink the ice in their drinks and gulp
into my thoughts
without a "*May I?*"

At today's requiem for two Jims,
the priest's cockneyed litany killed
initial *h* and left us
with a new language of grief:
oly, ome, ooh, and *ow.*

The oriole lays his notes upon us.
I resurrect the Santa Fe clay pot
and bury some rootstock at its loamy bottom.

Bix Biderbecke, Where Are You?

He died of everything. (1903-1931)

I sat by the rushes
where in dewy silence floated
lilies pink as evening sky.

Nearby I might have heard
his cornet,
its moaning mute against the bell,

the tone tonight, a luster
of intervals and swelling triplets
in one bar of *Jazz Me Blues.*

Last night Bix cued for *In a Mist*
as I was afield and peering.
There were ferns in the steely glade,

then splash of rain.

All Bitter Things

All bitter things conduce to sweet.
—Candide

To gloat,
perchance to vilify.
That was the glory!

That history,
that decadence
marked by the fork's golden tines,
must be amended.

I hereby apply for clemency.

De gustibus, I must repeat
before sending my apologies
downstream
on an index card.

When they arrive at port
in the Caribbean,
to be retrieved
by a passenger awash in the *vin ordinaire*
on the bold *Mermoz,*

how far I'll have come,
how sublimely my frostings
from bitter to sweet
will conduce.

When Peonies Bow

When peonies bow
I cut them; that grounds me.
The dinner bell calls, a door opens;
that holds me.
Rain freshens the vernal pool;
that instructs me.

Not so deep so as not
to deceive,
the basin fills.
I am satisfied to see crustaceans
in their ancestral home,
while I, like Ophelia, rest in mine.

Just when you think there was no actual
Ophelia,
she enters the room.
How one enters a room
is where the potential lies.

Want Not

Be always
in the company of music.
A cello will subdue
the scorpion's beating heart.

Like a rinse applied, bow takes to string,
no place can hide quicksilver.

Only three beats away from harmony,
what deception is there in a quaver?

Pushing forward, holding back,
tempo is seductive.

A suite of airs in chamber played
will wantonly subdue
the violins
as they pursue
the cello's beating heart.

from
SEA WIND ON THE WHITE PILLOW

(axes mundi press, 2009)

Undertow

Love you
as a mother, morning light,
linking motif, honoring direction.

And like a mother you reveal
that the way out to sea
is an aspect
of the way back to shore,
so over the billows I bound
unmindful of the whistle.

Blues to green-greys melt.
Waves beget waves
with sleek cut and curl.

A mighty trudgen crawl
is all I have against the swells
but there is cover
in the power of time.

When the last white crest weakens
into ripples behind me
and left wrist
thin-skinned where the pulse taps,
telegraphs its pain,

church bells call the hour.

I am not the first to pale
in frigid waters.

Innocence

At the house on the bay
where waves' wild thoughts fret the sea,
how unexpectedly a minor bruise
turns a faint pastel.

With every slight wind shift
there is a question,
and where I walk along the sand
bits of shell sink like so many yeses and nos.

Crabs take their sneaky promenades,
leggy brats waiting for a reprimand;
but there are no lessons in this haven
of sea and bells, terns plunging,
and sea wind on the white pillow.

He should have been jealous
of the sun
under which I drift and thaw, pure
in the rosy haze of July.

And as I drift, *Consequence*
becomes a boat, stunningly plain.

This Room, Through the Window

This room, through the window,
fills with ocean
and is unbounded.

I am sculling past all doors and all agendas.

White as a cheek, the ceiling peels to another white,
a bluish, then a bone.

There is ocean, nothing less,
a pulsing mirror through the window.

The tern's soprano breaks the briny egg
my heart has been.

The Venice of the Mind

I placed an X against my name
as if I were running for Viceroy
or Regent
or Tour Guide to Venice.

Psychological underpinnings aside,
I elected myself Tour Guide,
exulting in the chance to get away
from the steaming archipelago
of phony promises.

An empty suitcase is my relief,
mine to fill with other than
the day's tonnage....

Like the poison in absinthe,
I part slowly.
(Allegiance has its hold.)

On the train of thought to Venice
as *vaporetti* yield,
compromises are made.

Where there is speech,
there are echoes.

Tide's In: A Reverie

He draws a bath
by an open window,
sea breeze winnowing the water.
He lets the spigot murmur.

Or he enters at the beach
where I'm the one who's bathing
by the loofah and the sponge,
noon sun madding,
every balcony a beach chair.

He calls to me, shadows of birds
reminders that I've gone to meet the waves
and scan for dolphins astride
the horizon.

Tide's in,
never a lull in its flippant caress,
sea spray a misty relevance.

There's an exchange of birdcalls,
enough to tinge the blue,
but the substance is withheld
above the roll and suck of sea.

From Cake to Wafer

Yearly I come back to this big cake
of sky and sea to eat the honeyed particular
like a resident gull.

And I swear I know these other gulls
that wade, dip,
high-drop a clam a dozen times on the littoral
till I'm in so close!

They squawk (I am not Grendel's mother
but only want to cuddle), then desert me for golden rides
on corridors of air.

And I swear I know these other plovers
that at supper pipe their soft note as I intrude.

The truth is
I'm reeling with satisfaction; not self, but elemental.
I plunge into this salty bath, knowing it.

It's not indulgence, this cold deluge,
the icing of pure white sails promising communion.

All My Atlantics

Introduce me to these icy waves
as you would a baby. Dangle me
from your stronghold.
Tiny feet touch sea.
Inner screams. Mouth opens.
Lift
me.
Slip me in.

Under the surface
all sea life is in collusion
and of its murmur I am part.

Sound of surf and only that;
soft turbulence,
beloved incantation.

Ferris Wheel at the Seaside

I spin happily along,
lending muscle and lunacy
to a ride I never took before.

What an attitude, what a lift
I get, drifting in a circle that widens
as I go.

Who can blow this chance
to hit high and low together,
to sink and immediately rise
without years of preparation;
to crash and instantly
rebound,
silvery blue, everything round.

I've some crystal test tubes
to fill with seaspray, precious
as a fountain Coke.

I love a little fizz.

Boat Watch on Cape Ann

A yacht with parasol
goes by. I'm asked, *Miss
is this the Nile—*

that emerald
in Ethiope's ear?

I search the crown of a granite rim
for beach glass jewels
and tidal pools into which I peer
as trawler's circle.

Lobstermen cast an eye
as they slip their boats in and out
the harbor.

Schooners skim past, rending
my view of the horizon,
each sail pressed, a white rose
to the wind.

I can play back the whole regatta;
how the waves did lust and linger.

Where No Others

Wind and waves
in their awakening
carry my scheme like a bird
under the bridge and over the roiling water,
till I am marooned in a place
where no others
are of like audacity.

Among the salvage I can keep
a day-long still life pose;
or soothed by the muted scent of sea
never preen
but circle in my zone.

No inland view
inscribes itself upon my rock
as sea-wing does.

I fly above
the evergreen, the berm,
the chartreuse,
forming my intention soon to fulfill it,
bold as a jewel, raptor within.

Gazing with Galileo

What is it
about the stars in their mooring
that is so seminal?

In this nude space now dressed
with stars that shame
every other starry night in history,
what is as fresh?

Under midnight cover,
the moon spills an urn of polar light upon the water,
a Venice of nascent stars.

Ours is that telescopic view
of daughters
so mindful
of the fluid kick that connects us to the divine.

What is so provocative
about these unsheathed stars
that leave their shimmering imperative?

Awaiting the Hurricane: Three Women Bait the Hired Man

We carp about the winds
and moan from every window
that the sea has whitened.
Grasses press and coil against
the garden wall,
all its chinks expectant.

Our hired man
won't secure the porch stuff to the floor;
lies about the forecast,
tells Margaret she's controlling;
instead of boarding windows,
cuts the grass while hours pass.

He's lazy and remiss, cries Grace.
He's a pox upon the house.
Should I pack up and run away?

No. Stay poised
like a little rough tongue at the dish.

We'll nip corruption
at the garden gate. Our sultry perfumes
can coax this wasp to the Jell-O.

Breaking Camp

Rather than coerce some other habit
into the light, we dipped the canoe into
ever-blue reaches
following the textbook rendition of each cove.

Easily the currents flowed.
Better than any arrangement, they took us
downriver from Lake Tear of the Clouds,
showing mercy.

Now we've settled
in an old whaling town;
a few riffles on the river,
some flatwater days.

In ways the decades have of disappearing,
though boats still ply,
the break claimed for an evening
spread like a shadow into years.

Though *paddle* is a household word,
and the question's been raised,
our canoe
is an Old Town memory.

With vexing wax crayons
I blend blue and gray.
He factors in the zeal
with which we once played.

Small Pressed

Don't expect to find my verse
locked up in a drawer.
I'm not the moody interpreter anymore.
There's no stash to pocket.

Like a dolphin companion,
slick, synchronized,
in it for the fun,
I've run the paper strait—
every splash a dive.
Now to exchange the onion-skinned archives
for a right mind.

Mark this flowering ease.
Ever fewer nights torment.
The leaves are stabbed with starlight.

Acknowledgments

Grateful acknowledgement is made to the editors of the following publications in which these poems first appeared:

CLERESTORY

UCity Review: "The Less Lonely Perimeter," "Scenery"
Narrative Northeast: "Visit from a Raptor of Interest"
Unstamatic: "Alouette"
The Deronda Review: "Thoughts, Not Stories"
Right Hand Pointing: "Trinity"
Peacock Journal: "Clerestory," "Deconstruction," "The Art of Revision"

FEVER

Hamilton Stone Review: "X"
Waterways: Poetry in the Mainstream: "Sparring with a Reflection," "Little Philosopher II"
UCity Review: "Strength"
Blueline: "Frisson"
Right Hand Pointing: "Few Distortions"
Adelaide Literary Magazine: "Premonition," "Fierce," "Clarity," "Ease"

EQUAL PARTS SUN AND SHADE: AN ALMANAC OF PRECARIOUS DAYS

Cyclamens and Swords: "Against Breakage"
Right Hand Pointing: "The Lifesaving Properties of Solitude" (awarded the issue prize under the title "Three Things That Happened in March"), "Cruising," "Prisoner's Lament"
UCity Review: "Daily Bread and Cheese," "Infinity: An Epilogue"
Common Ground Review: "Company"

MINDING THE SPECTRUM'S BUSINESS

Blueline: "Momentum"
Cyclamens and Swords: "Light Lesson "
J Journal: New Writing on Justice: "Manners at the Round Table"
The Mochila Review: "Attitude," "The Tribe that Hid from Man," "Love Ever, Sam"

Poetry Storehouse: "Circumstantial Evidence," "All Rise"
Rabbit Poetry Journal (Australia): "Pes Anserine"
The Seventh Quarry Swansea Poetry Journal (Wales): "Swizzle Stick,"
    "Striking a Chord Across Time"
Waterways: Poetry in the Mainstream: "A Vague Unease," "Deep
    Attachment"

A STUDY OF EXTREMES IN SIX SUITES

Spillway Magazine: "Drella"
Assisi: An Online Journal of Arts & Letters: "Earth's Cries Recorded in Space"
The Caribbean Writer: "Penultimate Chapter"
Manifold Magazine of New Poetry (U.K.): "Spring Scat Song: An American
    in London"
Cyclamens and Swords: "Bix Beiderbecke, Where Are You?" "Want Not,"
    "The Adaptive Foe," "Litmus Test: The Work-Up"
Hudson River Art Magazine: "The Force of May," "A Little Bit Shy"
The Berkshire Review: "What Comes of Embrace"
Blueline: "Nearer"
Peer Glass Anthology: "Power and Potion"

SEA WIND ON THE WHITE PILLOW

The Berkshire Review: "This Room, Through the Window"
Connecticut River Review: "Gazing with Galileo"
Manifold Magazine of New Poetry (U.K.): "Where No Others"
Cape Cod Literary Press Anthology: "Awaiting the Hurricane: Three Women
    Bait the Hired Man"
Common Treasury: for poems set to music by composer Dallas Cline in an
    art song cycle of twelve poems for piano and voice, including "Ferris
    Wheel at the Seaside," "Innocence"

Cover photograph of peonies by Irene Mitchell; author photo by Jeffrey McMahon; interior and cover design by Diane Kistner; Gentium Book Basic text with Cronos Pro titling

About FutureCycle Press

FutureCycle Press is dedicated to publishing lasting English-language poetry books, chapbooks, and anthologies in both print-on-demand and digital (ebook) formats. Founded in 2007 by long-time independent editor/publishers and partners Diane Kistner and Robert S. King, the press incorporated as a nonprofit in 2012. A number of our editors are distinguished poets and writers in their own right, and we have been actively involved in the small press movement going back to the early seventies.

The FutureCycle Poetry Book Prize and honorarium is awarded annually for the best full-length volume of poetry we publish in a calendar year. Introduced in 2013, our Good Works projects are anthologies devoted to issues of universal significance, with all proceeds donated to a related worthy cause. Our Selected Poems series highlights contemporary poets with a substantial body of work to their credit; with this series we strive to resurrect work that has had limited distribution and is now out of print.

We are dedicated to giving all of the authors we publish the care their work deserves, making our catalog of titles the most diverse and distinguished it can be, and paying forward any earnings to fund more great books.

We've learned a few things about independent publishing over the years. We've also evolved a unique, resilient publishing model that allows us to focus mainly on vetting and preserving for posterity the most books of exceptional quality without becoming overwhelmed with bookkeeping and mailing, fundraising activities, or taxing editorial and production "bubbles." To find out more about what we are doing, come see us at www.futurecycle.org.

The FutureCycle Poetry Book Prize

All full-length original volumes of poetry published by FutureCycle Press in a given calendar year are considered for the annual FutureCycle Poetry Book Prize. This allows us to consider each submission on its own merits, outside of the context of a contest. Too, the judges see the finished book, which will have benefitted from the beautiful book design and strong editorial gloss we are famous for.

The book ranked the best in judging is announced as the prize-winner in the subsequent year. There is no fixed monetary award; instead, the winning poet receives an honorarium of 20% of the total net royalties from all poetry books and chapbooks the press sold online in the year the winning book was published. The winner is also accorded the honor of being on the panel of judges for the next year's competition; all judges receive copies of all contending books to keep for their personal library.